Pass The Blessing: Inspirational Quotes of Service and Encouragement

"The Faith Warrior"
Delleon McGlone

authorHOUSE®

AuthorHouse™
1663 Liberty Drive
Bloomington, IN 47403
www.authorhouse.com
Phone: 1-800-839-8640

First published by AuthorHouse 1/19/2011

ISBN: 978-1-4567-2865-6 (e)
ISBN: 978-1-4567-2864-9 (sc)

Library of Congress Control Number: 2011900467

Printed in the United States of America

Any people depicted in stock imagery provided by Thinkstock are models,
and such images are being used for illustrative purposes only.
Certain stock imagery © Thinkstock.

This book is printed on acid-free paper.

Because of the dynamic nature of the Internet, any Web addresses or
links contained in this book may have changed since publication and
may no longer be valid. The views expressed in this work are solely those
of the author and do not necessarily reflect the views of the publisher,
and the publisher hereby disclaims any responsibility for them.

Dedication:

To my Lord and Savior Jesus Christ, who has stood by me, guided me and loved me when I didn't love myself. For my mom who showed me that my relationship with God is the beginning to all my victories. To my Wife who loves me for me and my kids who motivate and inspire me, I love you. Thank you to anybody who has ever influenced me. Last but not least anybody who picks up this book: I wrote this book when God guided me out of my haze of darkness and depression and put me in a place of peace, calm, love and never ending blessings and positivity. I hope and pray you get something out of this to make you smile! PASS THE BLESSING!

Contents

FAITH FOLLOWER:

Having a vision of greatness and knowing and trusting that through any and all obstacles God will see you through

Start your day with renewed
FAITH and A renewed vision.

$\mathcal{F}$AITH is a doubt eliminator.

FAITH....that's my attitude and only the devil should have a problem with that.

Put yourself in the winners circle.
Having a Godly state of mind leads
to Godly actions also known as
Positive Results.

*J*ust like star athletes want the ball with the game on the line, you want God in your life all four quarters, overtime and especially with the game of life on the line.

*J*ust have FAITH… in your
FAITH.

If you can do anything at your peak you can definitely do anything to get out your valley.

You either CAN do or
YOU chose not to do but the
REALITY is it's up to YOU.

Plant (prayer) seeds with FAITH based soil and watch the results grow.

The size of the challenge is of know comparison to the size of your FAITH.

When the fridge is almost empty, the light bill is overdue, the rent checked is about to bounce know that you serve an on time God.

You can't claim what you don't own. So the only claims that we should really be making is the love of God whose grace and mercy keeps us blessed.

No Hope = No Faith, No Faith = Staying in the rat race. Much Hope = Much Faith. Much Faith = Striving for a better place.

Today is wonderful, beautiful, productive day and so is tomorrow cause you planed it that way in advance.

Worrying about what you can not control won't change the outcome, focusing on God will……Do your best and leave God to the rest.

Faith - Plan - Expectations -
Execute - Achieve. Move on to the
next goal with the same steps.

Faith + Prayer = Results You can't get one without the other. 1 + 1 = 2 not 3

*D*estiny is God given not man given. So don't let anyone get in your way (What God has for you let know one take away).

Whenever you feel the storm
clouds following you just PRAY for
the sun to shine through.

*J*ust believe in you…Nuff Said!

ACHIEVER BELIEVER:

Going after your ambitions with God as your shield and standing tall on your mountain top.

When you know how awesome
God is life is so much easier....I'm just
saying.

It's ok to start as the underdog
as long as you finish as the
OVERACHIEVER!

*L*imits....have none.

*L*ive your passion, life shouldn't be
any other way.

Expectations should never be realistic. You are the impossible dream that became the possible vision.

Your attitude is a reflection of you not of your situation. Think Big, Be Big, Achieve BIGGER!

God has already guaranteed you
the victory, what are you waiting for?

You get what you settle for, so only settle for the highest blessings God has for you.

If we work as hard for our needs
as we do for our wants we would
even our own playing field.

A fresh minted 100 dollar bill
& a wrinkly old 100 dollar bill still
have the same value & so do you.
God loves us when where up and
when where down. Our value doesn't
change in his hands. So your value
should be heaven high.

If you're always thinking positive and prosperous you won't leave room for the alternative.

*L*ife is not a box of chocolates but
it can be ;)

*D*ream it - See it - Work it -
Achieve it!

*N*ever give up on your dreams
unless you would rather live a
nightmare.

Life bumps and speed bumps are all the same. You just go over them and keep it moving.

$\mathcal{I}$'ve never met a successful
negative person…NEVER

Life obstacles are hard because the reward is that much greater.

Always think and be positive because the alternative is so not positive.

You will only get in life as much as you are willing to work for.

*M*ediocre effort mediocre result....

You are who you think
you are. That's either the
biggest loser or the biggest winner.
You are who you think you are! (I
repeated that for a reason).

THE BLESSED SEEK THE BEST:

*S*eeking first the kingdom of God and all the blessings that come with it

Your relationship with
God is the best customer
service you will ever find.

When you're empowered by God,
what else needs to be said? When
you're empowered by God it's easier
to get *ahead*.

The power of achievement & success is in YOU but only because God has given it to you, use it wisely.

*L*ife is full of intersections and highways, you're the driver, pick which way you want to go.

Failure doesn't exist. It's not a real word in any language.

*B*e encouraged and encouraging.
Being a blessing to someone else is a
blessing onto one's self.

Quitting doesn't exist. It's not a real word in any language.

Giving God the Glory for the small, medium and large things is the start to your victory.

Excuse don't exist. It's not a real word in any language.

You must have a valley
in order to start your peak.

Doubt doesn't exist. It's not real in any language.

You ever see someone
or hear a story about someone
changing their life? If it can be them,
it can be you.

God already sees the best in you so why are you still going through life with blindfolds on?

Accomplishment means the same
thing in any language.

God knows your heart but he also sees your actions. When you match up you add up.

Goals mean the same thing in
every language.

Even when you're trying to find yourself know that God has never lost you.

Successful people surround themselves with other successful people.

Delleon Mcglone

$\mathscr{P}$rogress can only be achieved through the work you put in it.

*W*hile being self encouraged,
encourage someone else…life
dominos.

You only have two options: Option A - live YOUR dream. Option B - live SOMEONE else's.

*N*ever be scared to take the attributes of people you admire and respect. Trust me they did and do the same thing. Who did Jesus admire?

L-O-V-E:

Self Love, being Loved, Spreading
Love, Showing Love, Loving
everything and everybody

Smile at a stranger, hug a friend,
kiss a love one, shine your light
bright for all to see.

$\mathcal{I}$ only see myself through the mirror of God and what looks back at me is TRIUMPH, SUCCESS, VICTORY, GREATNESS, FAVOR, BLESSING, GRACE, any and all things POSITIVE!

Positive energy is Godly energy,
anything else is wasted energy.

Love like there is nothing else to do.

How you treat yourself is how life
will treat you. So treat it great!

The world is a very big place; seek out its best parts.

You don't have to except where you are but you do have to believe in where you are going…See that Mountain Top!

*B*e humble and you won't have to
be humbled.

Take pride in who you are and grow from there. Even if you're not where you want to be, plant the seed and grow YOUR tree.

Positive energy is just like water it's
a need not a want.

Records are meant to be broken.
Be your own best record breaker.

Loosen up, make room for growth.

Delleon Mcglone

Prison of the mind is worse then prison of the body…BE FREE

New second, new start, new minute, new start, new hour, new start, new day brand new start.

Don't worry about the things you can't control, focus on the things you can control. FYI: Neither of those will ever change.

*D*on't be old to soon and smart too late. No time like the present....

Kindness is not weakness but weakness is not recognizing kindness.

*B*e a blessing to someone else just
cause....

Be a genie in the bottle of life and give someone three blessings.

Be a real-estate agent on positive street, positive blvd, and positive ave.

$\mathscr{B}$itterness is so sour, I'd rather be honey.

RR: Relax, Reposition and
Resurrect a new and better you.

Life is like a buffet, you pick what
you want.

Humanity has no color....

Self reward is the best reward. Work hard and earn the right to reward yourself....job well done in advance.

When you get on your knees and ask God for forgiveness be ready to forgive yourself.

*B*e of VALUE to you, for you,
about you and others like you.

We are all sinners who have God's grace and mercy.

EXTRA SUPPORT:

*A*dditional messages of Inspiration & Motivation

Anybody more blessed then me
is in heaven already! I call this
counting my blessing for all that has
been done for me.

*B*eing blessed is a spiritual State
of Mind.

God I love you for what you
HAVEN'T done for me....yet

What God has for you know
one can take from you but don't set
YOURSELF up to lose it.

We will all fall short of the glory of God but that is no excuse for not striving for excellence!

We lose parents, family, friends
& all kinds of other things but don't
ever lose the ORIGINAL source.
He's with you all the time.

Winners always expect to WIN.
Be of winning expectation!

*E*ven when we make mistakes God gives us another chance to make it right. TAKE ADVANTAGE OF THE ADVANTAGE.

For every mountain, for every valley you turned into a peak, Give PRAISE!